from professionals:

"I give a copy to each of my patients."
– Pediatrician/ G.W., M.D., Vallejo, CA

"I read it and want to buy a copy for my sister so she is ready when her 4 and 7 year olds enter puberty."
– Newspaper Reporter/ C.F., Sacramento, CA

"This is an excellent tool for parent and teen interaction. I wish it was available when I was parenting a teen male."
– Clinic Manager/ J.F., Elk Grove, CA

" ...a readable, thoughtful guide. It should go a long way toward easing kids and parents into and through a time which has for too long been associated with ignorance and apprehension."
– Physician/ Peter Bartlett, M.D.

" ...treats a difficult subject with frankness and clarity and yet with reverence...a model for parents and teachers and a valuable guide for youth."
– Lutheran Pastor/ Rev. Paul Hansen

from parents:

"I was pretty nervous but this book helped ME get ready to talk to my daughter."
– D.B., Sacremento, CA

"You've put together a most helpful and wonderful publication."
— E.J., Bodega, CA

"I found the book to be well developed and it lends itself to easy discussion between children and parents."
— J.F., Clovis, NM

"It's a great book. It made talking about sex with my daughter a positive experience and helped me feel comfortable. It covered all the topics and moral issues."
— E.M., Newington, CT

"It's the best book I've found for my 9 -year old son."
– S.U., Middletown, CT

from kids:

"I learned a lot about myself. Thanks." – Ronnie, 11 years old

"Talking with my parents about sex will not be as hard now." – Jennifer, 10 years old

Planned Parenthood®
Mar Monte

LET'S TALK
ABOUT
S-E-X

2nd edition

Book Peddlers
Deephaven, Minnesota
distributed to the book trade by PGW

Special thanks to:
Jeanne Ewy, Terrie Lind, Patsy Montgomery, Raul Tejeda and everyone who worked to bring this book back into print.

From an original work authored by Sam Gitchel and Lorri Foster.

Spanish Translation: Dori Kaplan

2nd Edition
ISBN 978-1931863-186
E-Book ISBN 978-1931863-575
(In Spanish, ISBN 978-1931863-193)

Publisher's Cataloging-in-Publication
(Provided by Quality Books, Inc.)

Let's talk about s-e-x / by Lorri Foster. -- 2nd ed.
p. cm.
Let's talk about sex.
Includes bibliographical references and index.
Audience: Grades 9-12.
ISBN 978-1931863-186
ISBN 978-1931863-193 (Spanish)

1. Sex instruction for children. 2. Sex instruction for youth. I. Foster, Lorri II. Title. III. Title: Let's talk about sex.

HQ53.G57 2005   649'.65
                           QBI33-2107

You can order a single copy of this book directly from the publisher. Schools, agencies, physicians office's, organizations, etc. can contact us for discount rates.

BOOK PEDDLERS, 18925 Lake Ave, Deephaven, MN 55391
952-544-1154
www.bookpeddlers.com

printed in Hong Kong
16 17 18   16 15 14

Let's Talk About S-E-X

**A Read-Together Book for
Kids 9-to-12 and their Parents**

with

A Parent's Guide

Planned Parenthood/Mar Monte

Contents

LET'S TALK ABOUT S-E-X

FOR THE
WHOLE FAMILY

Okay, here we go. The BIG TALK. No giggles, please. Do we HAVE to do this? YES. Why? Because you are growing up and will soon be a teenager. And because you don't always know what to ask and those older than you don't always know what or when to let you in on what you need to know. So we're starting the discussion here.

We all need to learn about sex and how sex fits into our lives. It's important that you get your facts straight. There is a lot of incorrect information floating around. Here are the things you may not know...and probably some that you do know. Now you can talk about sex and ask your questions. The adults in your life can share their feelings as well as what else you want to know. It's really just a beginning.

MAKING SENSE OF LOVE...AND SEX

When two people "fall in love" with each other, they want to be together a lot and want to share personal thoughts and feelings. They really care about each other's feelings, and they both feel good about themselves most of the time they are together.

Love and sex are not the same thing. "Love" is a word that people use to mean many things. We love our parents, and we love our pets. We love our close friends, and we love our grandparents. You might have even heard someone say "I love chocolate ice cream!" In each case the feelings are a little different.

In time, the excitement of falling in love may change to a deep feeling of love and trust for each other. Two people who share this kind of love usually want their relationship to last for a long time. They plan to work things out together. Whether times are good or times are tough, they know they can count on each other. For a couple like this, sex can be a way of expressing their loving feelings. Most people think this is the best time of a sexual relationship and leads to the best kind of marriage.

"Making love" is sometimes the term people use for having intercourse or sex (more about that later). But the fact is, love and sex don't always go together. Many people love each other without having sex, and others have sex without love. Some people have sex just for the physical pleasure they get from it or to please someone else. Others believe this is wrong, or just feel sure they would not enjoy sex without love.

To avoid problems everyone needs to remember that:
- No one has to have sex just to please someone else.
- Having sex will not make love happen.
- It is wrong to let someone think you love him or her when you really don't.

Of course, many people fall in love before they are ready for sex or for marriage. So it's a good thing that sex is not the only way to show these feelings. Other things, like being honest and really caring about one another, are more important in a loving relationship.

There are many ways, besides sex, to express feelings of love and closeness to someone. Doing special favors for the other person, being a good listener, holding hands, giving flowers…these are just a few ways.

Can you and your mom or dad think of some other ways of showing love? Try making a list:

_____
_____
_____
_____

How do the people in your family show love to each other?

_____
_____
_____
_____

Which of these ways would also be good ways of showing love to a boyfriend or girlfriend?

_____
_____
_____
_____
_____

MAKING BABIES

All living things reproduce their kind, and humans do this by having sexual intercourse. If we did not, the human race would not last long.

When a woman and man decide to make a baby, though, they are not usually thinking about the whole human race. They are looking forward to the joy of having and raising a child. Parenthood is a lifelong opportunity to love and care for another human being. It is also a lifelong responsibility. That's why deciding to make a baby is one of the most important decisions a person can make. Everyone who decides to have sexual intercourse needs to think very carefully about the possibility that a pregnancy could start.

Though making babies is important, it's not the main reason why couples have sexual intercourse. When two people care very much about each other, intercourse is one of the ways they can share their loving feelings. Joining their bodies in this special way gives them a special kind of pleasure which is why we do often call having sex, "making love."

Sexual intercourse may seem hard to understand. You may wonder, "Why would anyone do THAT? Why is 'having sex' such a big deal?" The answer is that sexual intercourse can add a lot of happiness to a person's life, or it can cause big problems. That's why it is a big deal. That's why it may seem that everyone is interested in it, or worried about it.

> **Q.** *Do you HAVE to have sex?*
> **A.** *Good question. NO, you don't.*

But we're getting ahead of ourselves. First we need to step back for a moment to understand how our bodies work before we deal with some of these larger issues. The better we understand what's going on within ourselves, the better we are able to make responsible decisions. Understanding can bring happiness—not problems—for us and those around us.

YOU ARE CHANGING ALREADY

If you are between 9 and 13 years old, there's something you should know about. It's something called PUBERTY. It's not as strange as it sounds. It's not a disease and it's not a tall building that must be leaped at a single bound. And it's definitely not a waste of time.

It might be happening right now; or it will be starting soon. One day you notice your body is starting to change, and you may think something is going wrong. Especially if no one has told you these changes are NORMAL. That's what this book is for: to let you know what kind of changes to expect.

WHAT IS PUBERTY?

Puberty is a few years of your life when your body and your feelings change very quickly. Puberty is a big step towards having the kind of body and feelings you will have as an adult. This period of rapid changing begins any time between the ages of 9 and 16, and lasts for 3 or 4 years.

You will keep changing all through your life – though probably a little more slowly after puberty. You won't wake up one morning and suddenly be an adult. Becoming an adult happens gradually. Keep reading and you will find out how.

EVERYBODY CHANGES

You've probably noticed that you and your friends are not all changing in the same ways or at the same time. Some kids get a lot taller before the other parts of their bodies catch up. Some get chubby, for a while, before their height catches up. But everybody gains weight. You're supposed to. You may hear a lot about too much extra weight (or looking fat). But not gaining enough weight can be a serious health condition, too.

A girl's breasts and hips grow larger, and so her waist looks smaller. A boy's shoulders grow broader, and he gets more muscles all over. Skin gets more oily, especially on the face. That's why some people get pimples (but keeping extra clean can help). Hair all over the body gets a little darker and coarser. It starts to grow in new places, like under the arms and around the sex organs. And the sex organs of both boys and girls get a little larger.

Along with these changes on the outside of your body, there are changes on the inside. The main ones are these: a girl becomes able to get pregnant, and the boy becomes able to make a girl pregnant. These are important changes.

WHAT IS NORMAL?

A lot of kids worry because they believe they are changing too soon or too late. If you're a girl, you may wish your breasts were larger or smaller. You may hope you don't start having periods much sooner or later than your friends.

If you're a boy, you may wonder about being too tall or too short, about the size of your penis, or about hair growing in places that it never grew before. Whether you are changing fast or slow, there's no need to worry.

Most girls begin the changes of puberty a year or two earlier than most boys. Anyone who starts much earlier than 9 or later than 16 should be checked by a doctor. The exact time your body will begin making these changes depends on your parents – if they started changing at a young age, you probably will, too. If they started later, that is probably when you will start.

Ask your parents if they can remember when their bodies started changing:

Did they start sooner or later than their friends?_____

At about what age?_____

What body changes did they notice first? _____

How did they feel about these changes? _____

What do they remember most about this time? _____

YOUR FEELINGS
...AND YOUR IMAGINATION

Growing up is not just a matter of your body changing. It also has to do with how you feel and the things you do. Most people have strong feelings during puberty: suddenly feeling excited, broken-hearted, loving, hating, angry, sad, happy, scared... maybe several different ways at the same time. Moods come and go, and you may not know why. You should know that it is not unusual for this to happen.

And you may think some pretty weird things now and then… wonderful things, awful things, some that could never really happen, and some that could. It is normal to imagine all sorts of things, even those you would never actually do.

There is nothing wrong with using your imagination. Daydreaming is one way to learn about yourself and think about how you might handle new situations. And there is nothing wrong with having a lot of different emotions.

But if your thoughts or feelings are keeping you unhappy, or taking up so much of your time that you can't do other things, you might want some help. Some good people to talk with are:
- your parents
- a counselor (your parents can probably help you find one)
- your minister, priest, rabbi or other religious leader
- another adult you can trust, such as your favorite teacher
- a local telephone hotline…look in the yellow pages of the phone book under "Crisis Intervention".

ACTING OLDER

Growing up also means doing new things. You will soon be old enough to do many things you couldn't do when you were a child. Many teenagers enjoy new experiences like wearing makeup, shaving, learning to drive, wearing "in" clothing, dating (or talking about it), or earning their own spending money. Some try things that are questionable like having body piercings and getting tattoos. Some even try things that are dangerous and can lead to serious trouble like experimenting with sex, alcohol, or drugs.

Teens try some things because they think it makes them look older. Smoking is one. But smoking is simply unhealthy and can be quite expensive when done on a regular basis. It can easily become an addiction (something which is terribly hard to stop even when you want to) and leads to serious health problems especially when you get older. You can save yourself a lot of trouble if you just don't start.

You will have a lot of decisions to make in the next few years. Many of your friends will begin to do new things, and you will need to decide whether to join in or wait awhile. Your parents can help you figure out when you are old enough for adult activities. Of course there are things that some adults do that your family may disapprove of at ANY age. Figuring out what's right for you will be easier if you know where your parents stand.

Which of the things have you discussed with your parents?

• teenagers learning to drive	• boys calling girls on the phone
• girls wearing make-up	• girls calling boys on the phone
• teenagers dating	• teenagers smoking cigarettes
• teenagers earning and spending money	• teenagers trying drugs and alcohol

Are there any others you want to add?

_____

_____

Which ones would you like to talk about now? _____

_____

_____

Ask your parents to tell you how things have changed since the time when they were growing up and note them here:

_____

_____

_____

THE INSIDE STORY

Puberty begins when your body starts to produce more of certain hormones. A HORMONE is a special chemical, which is made in a gland and released into the bloodstream. Hormones carry messages from one part of your body to another. Most of the hormones that start puberty come from a gland near the brain, the PITUITARY. These pituitary hormones tell the sex glands that it is time to start making some changes.

So the sex glands start making their own hormones—the sex hormones. Female hormones are made in the OVARIES, and male hormones are made in the TESTICLES. These male and female hormones cause the changes that are all part of puberty.

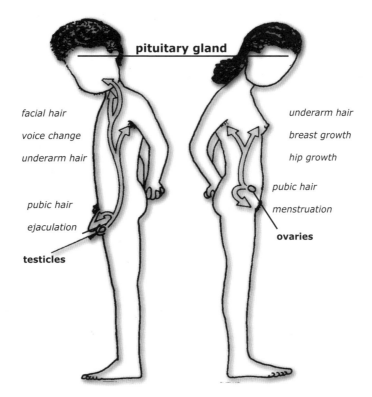

pituitary gland

facial hair
voice change
underarm hair

pubic hair
ejaculation

testicles

underarm hair
breast growth
hip growth

pubic hair
menstruation

ovaries

GROWING UP MALE

On the outside of his body a male has a PENIS and a SCROTUM. The penis is the part of a male's body which is most sensitive to sexual feelings. The scrotum is a thick pouch of skin that holds and protects the testicles. There is a narrow opening through the penis, called the URETHRA that urine and sperm travel through when they leave the body.

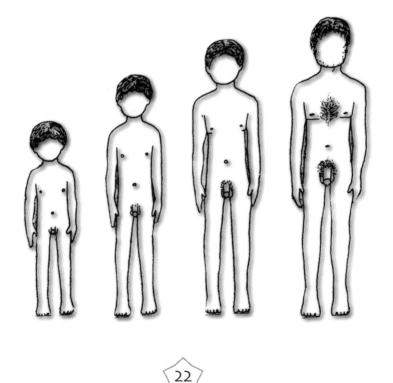

During puberty these parts grow a little larger and more sensitive. Many boys worry that their penis looks different from others. As a matter of fact, penises come in different sizes and shapes, just like feet, ears, and noses. One size and shape is as good as another.

All baby boys are born with a fold of skin, called the FORESKIN, partially covering the glans (tip) of the penis. Some parents have a doctor remove the covering right after birth, by a simple operation called circumcision. Other parents don't have it removed. Either way is fine. The only difference is this: males who have a foreskin should clean inside it when they shower or bathe.

During puberty a very important change takes place inside a boy's body: sperm cells start to be made. These cells are extremely tiny…seen under a microscope they look like skinny tadpoles. It's these sperm cells that cause a pregnancy. Every person ever born was started by a male's sperm cell joining with a female's egg cell.

Young sperm cells are made in the TESTES, or TESTICLES (both words mean the same thing), two oval-shaped glands inside the scrotum. After they mature the sperm cells move through two very narrow tubes, past glands located just above the scrotum. Here, other fluids are added, making a mixture known as semen.

Before we go any further, you should know about something that teenage males experience pretty often: erections. An ERECTION happens when extra blood fills spongy tissues inside the penis. The penis becomes larger and firmer, and sticks out from the body. (In spite of what some people say, there is no bone in the penis.)

When a male has an erection it is possible for semen to leave the body. EJACULATION is the way semen is released through his penis. This happens when muscles all around his sex organs contract several times, pushing the semen out through the urethra in a few little spurts. At the same time, he usually has a special tingly feeling called ORGASM, and his whole body feels really good. Of course, a male does not ejaculate every time he has an erection. (A drop or two of fluid may come out, though.) Whether he ejaculates or not, the erection will gradually go away.

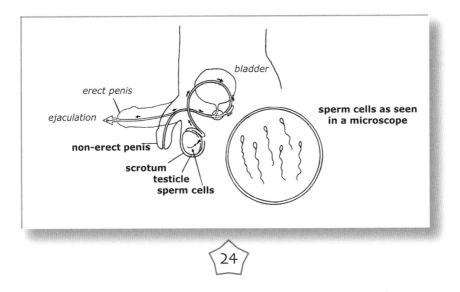

bladder

erect penis

ejaculation

non-erect penis

scrotum

testicle

sperm cells

sperm cells as seen in a microscope

All kinds of sights, sounds, and thoughts can cause an erection – even some that don't seem to have anything to do with sex. That's why erections can happen at unexpected times and places, like in math class or while watching TV. Almost all males have erections off and on while they're asleep, and many wake up with an erection. With each ejaculation, up to a teaspoon of semen is released. Surprisingly, this small amount of fluid contains an average of 400 million sperm cells. Even though semen and urine come out through the same opening in the penis, they are entirely different. Urine and semen cannot be released at the same time.

When the penis is fully erect the opening from the bladder closes, so no urine can come out. Ejaculation can be caused in several ways. Many boys have their first ejaculation while they are asleep. This is called a WET DREAM. They may remember having a dream about sex. Other times they won't remember any dream – there may just be a little spot on the sheet in the morning. This might be a little embarrassing, but most parents know that a wet dream is normal. It has nothing to do with accidentally wetting the bed. A wet dream is a healthy sign of growing up.

Q. Is it normal for one testicle to be bigger?

A. It is not uncommon for one to be slightly larger...and it is perfectly normal.

> ***Q.*** *How much hair will I get on my chest?*
>
> ***A.*** *This will depend on heredity. If your father has a hairy chest, you probably will too. When this occurs, however, differs from person to person.*

Another way boys may ejaculate is through MASTURBATION. When a male masturbates, he strokes or rubs his penis up and down in a way that feels good. There are many myths about masturbation and many slang expressions are used for it. The important thing to know is that masturbation doesn't cause any physical or mental harm. Don't believe stories that it causes boys to run out of semen or lose interest in girls.

Many people believe masturbation is a normal, healthy thing to do. Others just don't feel comfortable about it. They're not sure why – maybe because of something they were once told. And some people believe it is wrong for religious or moral reasons. But most people – young, old, married or unmarried – masturbate from time to time. And they all should know that it won't do them any harm, whether they choose to do it or not.

Males may also ejaculate when they have sexual contact with another person. One kind of contact is often called "making out." This means touching or being touched on the sexually sensitive parts of the body. Ejaculation can happen even without touching the penis directly. Another kind of contact is sexual intercourse. (We're getting to that soon.)

GROWING UP FEMALE

You may have noticed that for many girls puberty starts a year or two earlier than for boys of the same age. One of the first changes is in a girl's breast. Usually the nipple area will get darker and larger first. Then the fatty tissue that forms the breasts begins to grow.

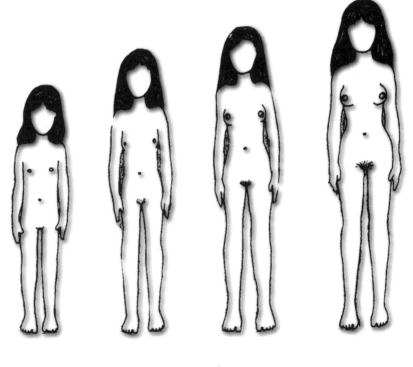

A lot of girls worry about the way their breasts look. Is one a little larger that the other? Are they too big? Too small? The wrong shape? It's easy to get this idea from TV and movies and magazines, that one, "perfect" figure is best for all women. Not true! Beautiful people come in all sizes and shapes. People who learn to appreciate their own special look have a happy self-confidence, which makes them likeable and attractive to others.

During puberty, a girl's hips grow wider, too. This makes her waist look smaller, giving her the curved body shape that most mature women have. Like breasts, some girls' hips grow a lot, and others grow just a little.

> *Q. Is it normal for one boob to be bigger than the other?*
>
> *A. Yes. No one has both of them exactly the same size. One may grow sooner than the other making this more noticeable.*

There are some other small changes which are not so easy to see, even though they are on the outside of the body. These changes are in the VULVA, a word that means all the sexual parts located between a girl's legs. During puberty all the parts of the vulva grow slightly larger and more sensitive.

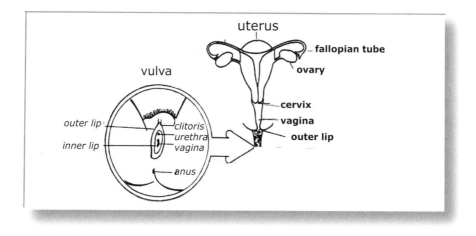

The outer part of the vulva – the outer labia or OUTER LIPS – is a protective covering for the rest. During puberty, hair grows on and around these outer lips. When the legs are apart, the outer lips separate so that the other parts of the vulva are uncovered. The inner labia, or INNER LIPS, provide another protective layer. Partly hidden by the inner lips, where they join at the top, is the CLITORIS. It is often covered by a little hood of skin, so only a small part can be seen. Like any body part, the clitoris comes in different sizes and shapes, but is usually no larger than a pea. The clitoris is the special part of the female's body, which is most sensitive to sexual feelings and touching. It gets slightly larger and firmer when a girl or woman feels sexually excited. In some ways, then, a female's clitoris is like a male penis.

If a girl or woman masturbates, she usually strokes this very sensitive area. She may also touch other parts of the vulva in a way that feels good. She may sometimes continue until she has an orgasm, the special tingly feeling of pleasure that both males and females can have. For a female, as for a male, masturbation does not cause any physical or mental harm. While some people believe it is morally wrong, others believe it is a good way for a girl to learn about her body and how it responds. Many females of all ages masturbate; others choose not to. Either way is normal.

Below the clitoris is the tiny opening of the URETHRA. As in a male, this opening is used for urinating. Below the urethra a female has a larger opening, called the VAGINA, which connects with the inside reproductive organs. Many girls have a thin ring of skin at the opening of the vagina, called the HYMEN. The hymen is small and hidden in the vaginal opening, so it cannot be seen in the drawing. Though it is just a partial covering, it may provide a little extra protection. An adult woman rarely has a complete hymen, because it usually has been stretched to the sides of the vaginal opening. This may happen during exercise, medical examinations, or while using tampons. If not, it will happen when she first has sexual intercourse. So you can see that a girl's hymen may be gone even though she has never had sexual intercourse.

Another opening located near the vulva is the ANUS. This is the opening for bowel movements, so, of course, males have this opening, too. While both males and females have a urethra and anus, females also have a third opening, the vagina. This is the opening for sexual intercourse, childbirth, and menstruation.

MENSTRUATION

A very important part of a girl's puberty is her first menstrual period. Menstruation, or "having a period" or "that time of the month" is a sign that her body is maturing, and she is becoming able to get pregnant.

Pregnancy is possible when an ovum (egg cell) is ripened and released from one of her ovaries. This happens about once a month, and is called ovulation. The ovum is very tiny – smaller that the head of a pin. After it leaves the ovary, the ovum moves down the Fallopian tube.

If a male's sperm cell reaches the Fallopian tube at this time, it will probably join with the ovum. This joining of egg and sperm is called fertilization. After the egg is fertilized, it continues moving through the tube, until it reaches the uterus. The uterus, also called the "womb", is an organ that every female has low in her abdomen (tummy). The uterus has a special lining, rich in blood and nutrients.

There, the fertilized egg can attach and grow. That is how pregnancy begins.

If the egg is not fertilized by a sperm, there is no pregnancy and the egg dissolves. The special lining of the uterus is no longer needed, so it breaks down and leaves the body. For about 3 to 7 days this menstrual fluid, made up of the blood-rich lining, comes out through the vagina. This is called menstruation.

A mature female menstruates about once each month. The average time, from the beginning of one menstrual period to the beginning of the next one, is 28 days. But it can range from 20 to 40 days for different women. When girls first start having their period, they sometimes skip a month, or even a few months, at a time. As they get older, most have their periods more regularly. But even adult women sometimes have late periods. Some things that can make a period late are:

- emotional stress
- great excitement
- sickness

- major changes in diet
- traveling or change in climate
- loss of sleep

A woman usually has no period while she is pregnant. Otherwise, menstruation usually occurs regularly until a woman is about 50 years old. Then she will gradually stop having periods and will no longer be able to get pregnant. This time in a woman's life is called menopause.

> *Q. My friends have gotten their periods. Is there anything I can do to hurry mine up?*
>
> *A. Sorry, no. Besides, you'll be having your period for many years so don't worry about rushing this process. While you may be anxious to grow up and be like your friends, each body matures at its own rate — the rate that is just right for your body. If anyone tells you they caused their period to start, it was just a coincidence, despite what they say.*

MORE ABOUT MENSTRUATION

To absorb the menstrual fluid, girls and women use either pads (sanitary napkins) to line their underwear, or tampons that are used internally to absorb the menstrual fluid. Both are made of absorbent materials, and are changed several times a day. They are sold in any drug store or supermarket.

Pads cover the opening of the vagina. Most kinds are held in place by an adhesive strip that sticks to the underwear. Tampons are worn inside the vagina. Many girls and women find them more convenient than pads. The muscles of the vagina hold them in place so they cannot fall out. And since the vagina is only a few inches long and ends at the uterus, a tampon cannot possibly be lost inside the body.

Deciding whether to use pads or tampons is a personal choice. Both come in a variety of types and sizes. Many women use pads sometimes and tampons at other times during their period. Girls might want to try several different products to find the ones they like best.

One word of caution: a disease called toxic shock syndrome (TSS) occurs most often among girls and women who use tampons. Although TSS is not fully understood, there are ways a girl or woman can protect herself from getting it. To be on the safe side, tampons should be changed at least once every six hours, and a pad should be worn, instead, for at least a few hours of each day during menstrual periods.

Girls who want to read more about taking care of themselves during menstruation can read one of the pamphlets or books listed at the end of this book.

Many girls feel glad when their periods first start, because this means that their bodies are growing and working normally. Others may at first feel that having periods is a "drag." Some people even act like menstruation is dirty or shameful, maybe because they do not understand it. While menstruating may sometimes seem inconvenient, it is a special womanly sign of a healthy body.

Most women feel fine during their periods. Some have a little discomfort during or just before. Cramping in the lower back or abdomen, slight weight gain, a feeling of heaviness, headaches, or feeling edgy and easily upset are common symptoms. Many girls have these problems less and less as they get older. A healthy diet and regular exercise may help, but if discomfort is really severe, a girl should see her doctor.

Normal Menstrual Cycle

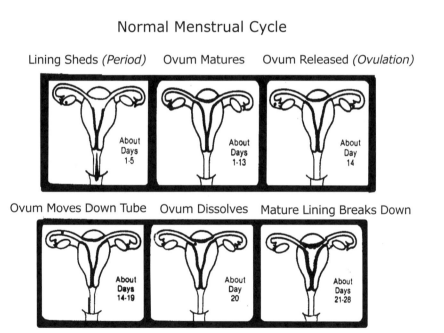

Lining Sheds *(Period)* Ovum Matures Ovum Released *(Ovulation)*

About Days 1-5 About Days 1-13 About Day 14

Ovum Moves Down Tube Ovum Dissolves Mature Lining Breaks Down

About Days 14-19 About Day 20 About Days 21-28

During puberty a girl may notice another change in her body. There may be a little bit of clear or whitish fluid in or around the vagina, or on her underwear. This normal discharge is the vagina's way of keeping clean, just as tears and saliva naturally keep the eyes and mouth clean. A small amount of fluid is always present in the vagina. A girl or woman may notice more moisture at certain times, especially around the time of ovulation, about a week after a menstrual period ends. Daydreams, night dreams, and exciting thoughts, as well as masturbation and sexual contact, can also cause extra wetness. If there is no itching, burning or other discomfort there is no need to worry. All this is perfectly normal.

SEXUAL INTERCOURSE

Now that you know about the bodies of both sexes, you can better understand what sexual intercourse is all about. From the illustrations you can see that the male and female sex organs are shaped so that they can fit together because one is an "inny" and one is an "outty." It is this fit that allows for sexual intercourse. That's it. It's really quite simple. But it's also quite complicated.

THE "WHYS"

In the right circumstances, sexual intercourse can be one of the most rewarding experiences a couple can have together. But it is not a simple matter, and you will find it easier to understand as you get older. For most people, having intercourse is a very personal thing, and belongs only in a close, trusting, and responsible relationship.

When a man and woman are attracted to each other, being close and touching can make them feel sexually excited. This means they have good feelings all over. The woman's vagina becomes more moist, and the man's penis becomes erect. When they feel this way, they may want to be still closer. If they decide to have sexual intercourse, they put their bodies close together, so that the men's penis can slide into the woman's vagina. This is actually pleasurable to both, and they continue moving in ways that feel good. They enjoy being as close as two people can be. Intercourse may last just a minute or two, or for quite a while, often until one or both has an orgasm. Usually the man's feelings peak (an orgasm), he ejaculates and his erection gradually goes away. After intercourse many couples continue to hold each other for a while, and enjoy feeling close. These intimate feelings are one reason why sexual intercourse can be so special.

> *Q. Does it hurt to have intercourse?*
>
> *A. No, it doesn't—or it shouldn't. If it's not a pleasurable experience, if someone is forcing you to have sex, or if you think there is a medical problem, you should definitely talk with your doctor or a health professional.*

Even though intercourse can give this unique pleasure, it's not as simple as it may sound.

AND...THE "WHY-NOTS"

Sexual intercourse is also how pregnancies get started. When the male ejaculates, his sperm cells are released in the female's vagina, and move toward her Fallopian tubes. If an egg cell is there at the time, it will probably be fertilized and a pregnancy could begin. But getting pregnant before you are ready to raise a child presents anyone with problems and decisions that can complicate one's life.

A few young people (approximately 1 in 5) have intercourse while they are still in their early teens. Most wait until they are older. For many reasons it's just smarter to wait. For one thing, some teenagers aren't ready for the emotional feelings and vulnerability that sexual intimacy can create and end up feeling hurt or upset. Also, having intercourse can create serious problems a young person isn't ready to deal with, like pregnancy and sexually transmitted diseases (STDs).

Q. *If you don't like it, do you have to do it again?*

A. *No. You have the right to say when and if you'll do it again.*

This book will tell you more about pregnancy and STDs. For now, just remember that anyone who has sexual intercourse needs to know how to prevent them. Some teenagers don't believe that pregnancy or STDs can happen to them. But they can — even the first, or only, time a person has intercourse.

There are other good reasons for teenagers to wait before they have intercourse. Why is it better to wait? Together with your parents, try listing some advantages here.

_____

_____

_____

_____

_____

_____

_____

_____

_____

_____

_____

PREGNANCY

So, pregnancy is started by sexual intercourse between a man and a woman. Now we will tell you about what happens between the time when the egg and sperm are joined and the time a baby is born.

Fertilization happens in one of the Fallopian tubes, at the end closest to the ovary. For the next 4 to 5 days, the fertilized egg cell continues to move down the tube until it reaches the uterus. This is where most of its growth will take place.

Pregnancy Cycle

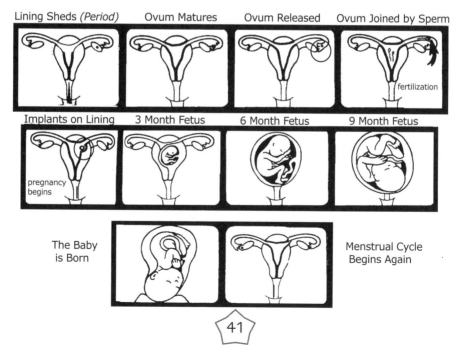

By the time the fertilized egg reaches the uterus, the blood-rich lining is ready to give it the nourishment it needs for growing. Within a few days, it attaches to the inside of the uterus (implantation) Here, it grows for about 9 months. Until the end of the second month it is called an embryo. From then until birth, it is called a fetus.

As the pregnancy develops, some remarkable changes happen within the woman's body. From the place inside the uterus where the egg is attached, the umbilical cord grows. This cord carries nourishment and oxygen, both needed for growth, from the woman's bloodstream to the bloodstream of the developing fetus. Since the fetus does not eat or breathe until it is born, everything it needs must pass through this cord. Also, the amniotic sac, a bag filled with watery fluid, grows around the embryo, and stays there throughout the pregnancy. This "bag of water" cushions and protects the developing fetus.

Of course, to make room for the growing fetus, the uterus must stretch a lot. During pregnancy, the uterus changes from the size of a pear to the size of a small watermelon. Naturally, the pregnant woman's shape also changes to make room for her growing uterus. After the baby is born, the uterus gradually shrinks back to the size it was before pregnancy.

CHILDBIRTH

After about nine months of pregnancy, the mother gives birth to her baby. With each passing month, the fetus has become closer to being ready for birth and able to survive outside its mother's body. When the time for birth is near, the mother feels the muscles of her uterus firmly squeezing every few minutes. This is referred to as "going into labor." As the squeezing gets stronger, the cervix (the opening at the bottom of the uterus and at the top of the vagina) gradually stretches open more and more. This may take a few hours or many hours during which her body is working hard to allow the baby to be delivered. During this time, the mother tries to stay relaxed while the muscles of her uterus work hard to open and then to push the baby out. Finally, the cervix stretches open wide enough for the baby's head to pass through.

Then the mother begins to push down, as hard as she can, with the muscles of her abdomen. Her effort combines with the squeezing of her uterus to push the baby into the vagina, usually head first. Then within minutes, the baby slips from the mother's body into the outside world.

When a baby comes out, it is still attached to its umbilical cord. Now that the newborn can start breathing and eating on its own, it doesn't need this connection any more. Soon after birth, the cord is cut, close to the baby's tummy. Cutting the cord is painless, and the small cut will soon heal. The short piece of the cord dries up and falls off. What remains becomes your navel, or belly button. Everybody has a navel where their umbilical cord used to be attached.

Is there anything you would like to ask your mom or dad about your own birth? Maybe they even took pictures of your delivery. Write your questions as well as their answers here. You can use these for starters : (what time of day did your mom go into labor?; was her labor short or long?; were you born in a hospital?; was your father in the delivery room with her?):

_____
_____
_____
_____

Childbirth usually takes place the way we have described, but occasionally something unusual happens. If you are interested in some of the unusual things, you and your parents might want to do some reading in a good book or encyclopedia. Some interesting things to learn about are: twins, triplets, Caesarean section, breech birth, and premature birth.

Q. How do twins decide who will come out first?

A. They flip a coin? I don't think so. Seriously, it's just a question of timing and positioning—though the first one out is forever the "oldest".

While a woman is pregnant, her breasts get ready to make milk for feeding the baby after it is born. Shortly after the birth, hormones are released as a signal so that the breasts begin to produce this milk. Most babies are able to suck from their mother's breasts soon after birth because sucking is an instinct they are born with. Many mothers enjoy feeding their babies this way. Breast milk is a complete and nourishing food for a newborn for many months. It is best for a baby but, for one reason or another, a mother may prefer or need to feed her baby with a bottle of a baby milk formula. Either way is fine.

Which way were you fed when you were an infant?

_____

How long did you drink milk before you started eating other foods?

_____
_____

What was your first solid food after milk as a baby?

_____

HEREDITY...What Makes You, YOU

What makes one person tall and another short? Why do some people in the same family look alike, and others look different? Why do identical twins look alike? Why do dogs give birth to little dogs, and cows have little cows, and humans have little humans?

Inside every cell of every living thing are many chromosomes. These chromosomes carry the master plan for how that plant or animal will grow. The shape of your nose, the color of your skin, and the type of hair you have are all controlled by your own individual set of chromosomes.

All humans get half of their chromosomes from the father's sperm and half from the mother's ovum. Since the child only gets half of each parent's master plan, some parts are included and some are left out. That is why most children look something like their parents, but not exactly like them.

Every man has some sperm cells that carry a "female" chromosome and others that carry a "male" chromosome. Whether a new baby is a girl or a boy depends on which type of sperm fertilized the mother's ovum.

HAVING SEX WITHOUT HAVING A BABY

So now you know quite a bit about puberty. You know that puberty means your body will change to an adult body, capable of reproducing. You know that all through life everyone has sexual feelings and that these feelings grow stronger during puberty.

And you know the process of how a baby is made, how it grows during pregnancy and how it is born.

Often a couple has intercourse even if they do not want a baby right then. Some people prefer to have no children. Some prefer to wait until a time when they can better care for a child. Some already have a number of children they want. These couples use some kind of birth control (contraception). By using contraception, a couple can have intercourse and be reasonably sure they will not start a pregnancy.

One kind of birth control you probably have heard about is the contraceptive pill (or just "the pill"). You might also have heard of condoms ("rubbers"). There are several other ways to prevent pregnancy, each with its own advantages. One way or another, they all work by preventing the egg and sperm from getting together and growing in the uterus. Some methods are prescribed by doctors or clinics, and some are sold in drugstores without a prescription. If you want to find out more about different methods of contraception, see the reading list for some suggested books.

> **Q.** *What is a condom? Is there a female condom?*
>
> **A.** *A condom is a latex (rubber) covering that fits snugly on an erect penis that will hold male sperm. There are a variety of condoms and they are readily available in many different kinds of stores. Yes, there are also condoms designed for females but they are not as common and you may only find them in health clinics.*

MAKING LOVE (without making mistakes)

Many teenagers face a lot of pressure to have intercourse before they are ready. Sometimes teens think that everybody else is doing it. It's easy to get this from TV shows, movies, and big-talking friends.

But the truth is, most teenagers are not having sex. Most TV shows and movies use sex for one simple reason: it gets attention and makes money. But these shows rarely show life as it really is. And friends who try to get you to have sex are not thinking about what's best for you.

There are some important things that TV, movies, and friends usually leave out. For one thing, making love involves our most intimate feelings. Being this close with someone before you are ready can leave you feeling embarrassed, hurt, or used. Adding sex can make a nice relationship complicated and difficult.

There are many STDs (sexually transmitted diseases), too. You may not have heard of some of them but they are very much around. Some common ones, especially with teenagers, are chlamydia, herpes, genital warts, and gonorrhea. Each one causes different problems, such as sores or damage to internal organs that can limit your chance of having a baby when you are ready to have one. STDs are passed from person to person when they have sex—even oral sex.

Anyone who has sex needs to know how to avoid getting a sexually transmitted disease. The most serious STD is HIV/AIDS, a disease caused by a virus (the human immunodeficiency virus, or "HIV"). AIDS attacks the body and keeps it from being able to fight off other diseases. Nearly everyone with AIDS needs intensive medical care to prevent serious complications, including death. Sex and the sharing of bodily fluids is one of the ways that people get HIV. Other ways are sharing needles to shoot drugs, and during childbirth if the mother is infected.

What makes this so hard to take seriously is that a person may be infected without showing any signs of the disease for weeks, months, or even years. This makes it much easier for these diseases to spread, because people often have the germs without knowing it. The only way to be sure is to go to a doctor or clinic for testing. There are treatments for all STDs so anyone who might have one should be checked as soon as possible.

Of course, the best thing is to protect yourself from getting an STD in the first place. There are several ways to do this. One way is not having sex. STDs can only be caught through close contact with someone who is already infected. As long as you don't have sex, you won't get a sexually transmitted disease.

Someday, though, you will probably want to have a relationship that includes sex. When you are mature and ready for this, you can protect yourself by having "safer sex." Safer sex means EACH person uses a birth control method. It also means being as certain as you can that the person you have sex with is not infected. You will need to be able to talk with that person about all of this, and you will need to trust that person.

What kind of person do you imagine would have an STD? In fact, all kinds of people get them. You can't tell by people's clothes, or who their friends are, or where they live. You can only tell by knowing someone very well, talking about STDs, and trusting that person to know about STDs and to be honest with you.

You can see there are lots of things you need to know before you're ready for sex. Learning about STDs and safer sex is one part. Learning about birth control is another. You also need to understand yourself. And you need to be able to be a good partner. That's a lot to learn, but you have plenty of time. Don't let anyone push you before you're good and ready.

How do you know when you can trust someone? See if your parents can help you figure this out.

ARE YOU READY FOR A BABY?

Being a good parent is one of the toughest jobs in the world. It takes a lot to be ready for parenthood. Try listing the five most important qualities you think parent needs to have, and ask your mom or dad to do the same:

Your List:

_____

_____

_____

_____

_____

Your Parent's List:

_____

_____

_____

_____

_____

If you are not ready to have a baby, you are not ready to have unprotected sexual intercourse.

GOOD START

So now you know more about puberty. You can see it has a lot to do with sex and reproduction. These are big subjects, and there are a lot of other interesting things to know. By sharing this book, you and your parents have made a good start. But any book covers only a small part of all there is to know. Hopefully you will continue to talk and learn together.

There may be other things you are wondering about. Some real questions by preteens have been asked throughout this book. There is no such thing as a stupid question. If you have questions, list them here:

_____
_____
_____
_____
_____
_____
_____
_____

Now that you are almost a teenager, ask your parents if there are other things that they would like you to know. Write their answers here:

_____
_____
_____
_____
_____
_____

During the next few years you will learn a lot more about understanding yourself and others. From each new person you get to know, you will learn more and more about what you want from a close relationship. No one knows this ahead of time. Learning about love and sex continues all through life.

THE PUBERTY PUZZLE

All the answers to this crossword puzzle come from the parts of this book that you have just read. Fill in the answers you know, and ask your parents for help with the ones you're not sure about.
(The correct answers are shown on the bottom of the next page.)

Across:

3. The male sex cell which can fertilize an ovum is called a_____cell.
6. When a male's penis becomes larger and firmer, this is an_____.
7. The _____produce female hormones and store egg cells.
8. The_____produce sperm cells and the male hormone.
10. An_____is released from the ovary about once a month in mature females.
12. The female organ that is most sensitive to sexual feelings is the _____.
13. _____are produced in the sex glands of both males and females and cause the changes of puberty.

Down:

1. A fertilized ovum (egg) attaches and grows in a woman's _____.
2. The male organ that can become erect is the _____.
4. About once a month the lining of the uterus breaks down and leaves the body. This is called _____.
5. The opening where this menstrual fluid comes out of the body is the _____.
9. The _____ is the thick pouch of skin that holds a male's testicles.
11. _____ is the special tingly feeling of sexual pleasure in both men and women.

More Good Books for You

What's Happening to My Body? Book for Boys
What's Happening to My Body? Book for Girls
By Lynda Madaras (Newmarket Press, 2000)
My Feelings, My Self; A Growing-Up Guide for Girls
By Lynda Madaras (Newmarket Press, 2002)
Ready, Set Grow: A "What's Happening Book to My Body?" a book for younger girls
By Lynda Madaras (Newmarket Press, 2003)
Changing Bodies, Changing Lives: A Book for Teens on Sex and Relationships
By Ruth Bell (Three Rivers Press, 1998)
The New Teenage Body Book
By Dr. Kathy McCoy and Dr. Charles Wibblesman (Perigee, 1999)
It's Perfectly Normal: Changing Bodies, Growing Up, Sex & Sexual Health
By Robie Harris (Candlewick, 1996)

Boys and Sex
By Joely Carey (Barrons, 2002)
From Boys to Men
By Michael Gurian and Brian Fioca (Price Stern Sloan, 1998)
The Guy Book: An Owners Manual
By Mavis Jukes (Crown, 2002)
What's Going on Down There? Answers to Questions Boys Find Hard to Ask
By K. Gravel (Walker & Co, 1998)

The Care & Keeping of You: The Body Book for Girls (American Girl Library)
By Valerie Schaefer (Pleasant Company, 1998)
PERIOD. A Girls Guide
By JoAnn Loulan and Bonnie Worthen (Book Peddlers, 1979 & 2001)
Deal With It! A Whole New Approach to Your Body, Brain & Life as a Gurl
By Ester Drill, H. Mcdonald, R.Odes (Pocket, 1999)

This Book is About Sex
By Tucker Shaw and Fiona Gibb (Puffin, 2000)
What's the Big Secret? Talking About Sex with Girls & Boys
By Laurie and Marc Brown (LittleBrown, 2000)
Where Did I Come From?
By Peter Mayle (Citadel, 2000)

Websites for Teens and Preteens

www.teenwire.com
Sexuality and relationship information from the trusted organization of Planned Parenthood Federation of America (PPFA). This award-winning website is specifically designed to appeal to teens and contains accurate, factual information and interactive activities and quizzes that are updated frequently. Information is available in Spanish or English and is reviewed by a panel of experts.

www.itsyoursexlife.com
The website's primary purpose is to provide reliable, objective sexual health information to young adults. There is also a section specifically targeted to parents. Content is reviewed by a panel of outside experts and is funded by The Henry Kaiser Family Foundation. Information is available in English, Spanish, French and Arabic.

www.sxetc.org
This website is directed by teens for teens. It contains articles containing factual information written by teens, quizzes and other interactive features. The site is sponsored by Rutgers University, Network for Family Life Education. There is also a free downloadable monthly newsletter for teens.

www.gURL.com
This website is an on-line community and content site for teenage girls. It contains stories, games and interactive content on a broad range of topics that appeal to girls.

www.kidsgrowth.com and www.teengrowth.com
These related websites were established and are maintained by a team of pediatricians to provide factual health information to teenagers. The site uses an attractive format, but the content is presented in a more formal manner than some other sites.

INDEX for the
Read-Together Book

Planned Parenthood®
Mar Monte

A Guide for Parents
and Other Trusted Adults

for

Let's Talk About S-E-X

about using this book

This guide book is written for parents, guardians and other trusted adults who care for children – their own or those placed in their care. The words "son" and "daughter" were chosen to reflect a trusted relationship and not to imply a biological connection. The information contained in this book can help you and your son or daughter talk more comfortably about sex. This part is for you. It will help you get ready to talk with your child about the information in the rest of the book. The first part of this book is for your pre-adolescent girl or boy to read and discuss with you. It gives factual information about growing up. Perhaps more important, it also includes interactive ways which will help you discuss your family values and beliefs. Children need to understand your values, and you are the best person to explain what you believe. Sharing together the information here can open the door to more honest communication as your children enter their teenage years.

WHY PARENTS AND YOUTH NEED TO TALK

Our youth learn about sex every day. Television, bathroom walls, billboards, playground jokes, and popular music all give them messages about sex. Unfortunately, most of these messages are not very helpful. They usually don't explain basic facts. They almost never show the responsibilities that go along with sex, and may lead children to think that sex is a carefree game.

Sometimes school programs can help. A few schools do offer comprehensive sexuality education courses. These programs not only provide important factual information; they also help students learn to understand themselves and make responsible decisions. Most schools, though, provide only two or three lectures that cover some basic facts about reproduction and sexually transmitted diseases. While this information is valuable, many students' questions remain unanswered. Even if your child is lucky enough to have a good school sex education program, nothing can replace the kind of teaching parents can offer. As a parent you can give your child information in a personal way and at the times that best meet his or her needs. And no school program can teach your family values, the particular beliefs that you want to pass along to your child.

Of course, children have already learned a great deal from their everyday experiences as part of their family and community. From the way they are fed, held and comforted as infants, they learn about closeness and physical affection. From relationships with family and friends, they learn about caring and responsibility. From their parent's way of handling their squabbles with others, they learn about sharing and consideration. From listening to the way parents talk with each other and other family members, children learn about love, communication, and getting along in a close relationship. All these experiences, and many others, will influence their attitudes, feelings, and behavior, now and in the future.

Even though so much learning takes place without words, it is still important for families to talk about sex. A child who has correct information and a clear sense of family values is more likely to make careful decisions. Parents need to show that they are willing to talk, rather than waiting for their children to come to them with questions. Avoiding the subject may suggest that sex is too difficult, too embarrassing — or perhaps too dirty to be talked about. This makes it even harder for children to ask for the information they need. They may be left with only the hodgepodge of ideas they pick up outside the family.

A GOOD TIME TO TALK

A very good time to build family communication about sex is when your child is between 9 and 12 years old. At this age most children are very interested in trying to understand how everything works, including their own bodies. Despite a common exterior of embarrassment, sex is a topic children are VERY interested in. They often try to figure out sex and reproduction in the same matter-of-fact way they might try to understand how an automobile engine works.

As their own bodies, or their friends' bodies, begin changing, preteens become very interested in what is normal. Since some begin to develop early and others lag behind, many youngsters are very concerned about being different from their friends. Talking with parents can help to reassure them that these differences are completely normal.

This is also an excellent time for parents to begin discussing their values and beliefs about issues such as dating rules, "dirty jokes," sex before marriage, etc. Few preteens are ready to carry on long discussions on such topics. But they are likely to remember what you say if you keep your remarks simple, specific, and do not insist that they immediately agree.

As youngsters become teenagers, talking about sex usually becomes a more difficult topic to discuss with parents. It is normal for teenagers to want more independence and some distance from their own families. They need a reasonable amount of privacy and trust. Also, as their sexual feelings become stronger, they may be less able to discuss sex in the straightforward way of the pre-adolescent. But if you have already established a pattern of honestly talking about sex-related topics, it is more likely that you will be able to continue this communication through adolescence.

YOUR OWN DISCOMFORT

All parents feel at least a little uncomfortable talking to their children about sex. Maybe your parents never talked with you about sex, so you feel unsure about what to say. Maybe you are worried that you don't know the answers to all the questions that might come up. Nobody does. Feeling uncomfortable doesn't have to stop you from talking. This may even be an opportunity for you and your children to find the answers together. There are some things you can do to help feel more at ease, though.

First, review the information contained in this book. Think about what you will say when your child asks you questions. Maybe you will want to discuss your answers ahead of time with your spouse, partner, a close friend, a relative or a health professional. If you want to read more about certain topics, you could try some of the readings listed at the back of this book.

Just the idea of saying some of the words in this book, words like "penis" or "vagina" may make you feel uncomfortable. You might want to practice saying them to yourself, possibly in front of a mirror, before you try talking with your child. You may feel a little silly at first, but with practice this feeling will wear off. If you do feel embarrassed when you try to talk, you can admit this honestly to your son or daughter. Almost everyone feels that sex is a special, private subject. Admitting your own discomfort will probably help you both feel more comfortable.

You may also want to do an informal review of the language you use. Children pay attention to the words their parents use and imitate those words, even when they do not fully understand them. Using words that are hurtful or disrespectful such as "fag," or "bitch" or other harassing words will be confusing to children because these words are disrespectful and damaging to others. Sex is about respect and caring, not harassment, coercion or making others feel bad.

Finally, you don't have to do this all alone. You can certainly include your spouse or another trusted adult. There will be times when both adults together can be involved in talking, or each can talk to the child separately. Even having conversations with an older sibling present can expand the scope of your discussion with a younger child.

Many parents wonder if it is okay for a mother to talk with her son about sex or for a father to talk with his daughter. The answer is YES. In fact, sometimes talking with a parent of the opposite sex has special advantages. Most pre-teenagers and early teenagers are very interested in how other people see them, especially people of the other sex. The opposite-sex parent can give this viewpoint. For example, a mother can help her son understand how women think and feel about men. She can help him to understand and respect girls' thoughts and feelings. After all, she was once a girl herself!

Mothers are usually more willing than fathers to discuss sex with either boys or girls, but fathers also have a lot to offer children of both sexes. Encourage a father's participation by sharing this book with him as well. Still, it is a parent's willingness to talk and to listen which is much more important than which parent happens to be talking about sex.

HOW MUCH DOES YOUR CHILD NEED TO KNOW?

Like most other parents, you may wonder what topics you need to discuss with your preteen. The following checklist includes the basic topics that all children, both boys and girls, need to know about in order to understand the changes of puberty. These are explained in detail in this book.

It is not easy for most parents to talk about sex. But discussing these topics frankly at the right times can help your child to grow up with more confidence and less worry about normal feelings. Your willingness to talk openly about these subjects will make it easier for your child to come to you as the teen years bring new interests and concerns.

MALE & FEMALE BODIES
    __ Male sexual and reproductive organs, internal and external
    __ Female sexual and reproductive organs, internal and external
    __ Physical changes of puberty, male and female
    __ How these changes relate to reproduction
    __ That these changes bring about new feelings and emotions
    __ That people mature at different rates

MENSTRUATION
    __ What it is
    __ When it occurs
    __ That it is normal
    __ How to be prepared

ERECTIONS & WET DREAMS
    __ What they are
    __ That they are normal

MASTURBATION
    __ What it is
    __ That it is not harmful
    __ That it is normal to do it—or not to do it
    __ Your family's feelings about it

SEXUAL INTERCOURSE
    __ What it is
    __ How it is related to pregnancy
    __ Your beliefs about how it relates to love, marriage, birth control, etc.

RISKS
    __ Sexually transmitted diseases
    __ Unintended pregnancy
    __ Hurt feelings
    __ Relationship problems

Are there other things YOU consider important, which are not included in this checklist, but which you want to be sure your child understands? The spaces below are left for you to add these topics. Make notes here about other topics you want to bring up.

_____   _____

_____   _____

BUILDING SELF-ESTEEM

Helping your child feel good about him or herself is probably the most important influence on your children's sexual development. As they become teenagers your children will be faced with many difficult and important decisions. People who feel good about themselves are less likely to let others pressure them into making unwise choices, and don't need to use others to make themselves look good or feel good. They are more likely to make responsible decisions about sex, and about many other things as well. Here are some things you can do to help your children feel good about themselves.

Let them know that you appreciate them.

Recognize their talents, personality, looks, accomplishments and anything else you can think of. Avoid comparing them with others. Help them discover their own special strengths.

Treat them with respect.

Ask for their opinions. Listen to their ideas and feelings. Think about what they say to you. Don't cut them off, even when you disagree with what they are saying, hard as that can be. Hear them out. Their self-respect begins with the respect and consideration they receive from you and others.

Teach them to set proper boundaries.

Teach your children that there is "good touch" and "bad touch." Help your children learn that they have the right to choose who touches their bodies. They can tell other children and adults that they do not want to be touched and they should expect that others would respect their wishes. Encourage them to talk with you if they feel that someone has touched them inappropriately or made them feel uncomfortable. Help girls, especially, understand that their facial expression and body language need to match the words "no," "don't," or "stop that." If one giggles or laughs, one sends a message that they are not really serious. You can not say a real "NO" with a smile or a giggle.

Don't expect too much or too little.

Many youngsters feel insulted because they think their parents treat them like kids. Others get discouraged because they feel their parents expect more than they can do. It is important to let them know that you have confidence in them. You can support them without pushing. You can protect them without keeping them from new experiences.

Avoid too much criticism.

Preteens and teens are extremely sensitive to criticism. If they hear too many negatives they may just stop listening. They often do want to hear parents' opinions, when expressed tactfully and with love. And when your children fail at something or make a mistake, let them know that it is not the end of the world.

LISTENING IS IMPORTANT

To TALK to your children in a way that will really help, you have to also LISTEN to their words, and to the feelings behind their words. You must try to see things through their eyes. If they feel that you understand them, they are more likely to talk openly with you. One of the best ways to see the world through your child's eyes is to try to remember yourself at the same age.

Spend a few minutes thinking about these questions:
- When did you notice your body starting to change, and how did you feel about it?
- What ideas did you have that were mistaken?
- What did your parents tell you about sex?
- At what age?
- What did they say that was helpful? What was not helpful?
- What do you wish they had said or done to help you understand yourself and others?
- What do you want to do in the same way with your children?
- What do you want to do differently?

Some of the things our children go through will be similar to things you experienced when you were young. Others will not be. It may help to relate a few stories of your own experiences. The danger is in going too far, saying "I know exactly what you're going through" about everything. Young people are quickly turned off by this approach. Careful listening also makes it easier for you, because you will have a better idea about exactly what your child needs to know. Before answering a difficult question, it may help to ask your child what he or she thinks the answer is. The reply may tell you what you need to say next.

For example, a pre-adolescent might ask: *"Dad, why do people have sex?"* What does that child mean when she says "sex?" Kissing? Making out? Sexual intercourse? And even after you find out what she means by "sex," there is more than one answer because people have sex for a number of reasons. Probably this preteen heard or saw something specific that triggered the question.

You might say:
"There can be different reasons. Why do you think people have sex?"
     "I don't know…(silence)…well…Suzanne said people have sex when they love each other."
"What do you suppose she means…'having sex'?"
     "I don't know…I guess kissing and stuff."
"Yeah…anything else?"
     "Well…she said something like…'inner'…uh…'innercourse,' I think."
"She was probably talking about sexual intercourse—"
     "Yeah, that's it…"
"We sometimes call it 'making love.' That's because when a man and a woman love each other, they like to get as close together as possible. They may decide to have sexual intercourse. The man's penis fits inside the woman's vagina, and –"
     "Oh, yuck…why would they want to do that?"
"It may sound strange to you now, but at the right time it can be a really nice way of showing love, and it feels good to both people. You will understand those feelings better when you're older."

"How old do you have to be?"
"Well, people have different ideas on that. Your mom and I believe it's best to wait until you're married. For one thing, when people have intercourse, the woman could get pregnant…"

By gently asking a few questions, this father was able to talk with his daughter about the things she really wanted to know. A hasty, preachy answer might have cut off the conversation. He showed that he was willing to talk and listen, so his daughter asked more questions.

All things cannot be covered in one sitting. And some things will probably need to be brought up more than once and you might find the same conversation may even get repeated. There is no need to sit down and have a BIG SERIOUS TALK. The best way to talk about sex is in the everyday conversations that are a natural part of family life. Take advantage of opportunities that spark such conversations.

FACTS AND VALUES

Your child needs to know both the facts about sex and your family values. Facts are facts. They are the same for everyone, whether we like them or not. Values are different for different people. Our decisions about what we like or dislike, what we approve or disapprove, are based on our individual values as well as our family's cultural heritage. For instance, it is a fact that a lot of unmarried people are having sex these days. We may or may not think it's right, according to our values. But it is still a fact.

Preteens will soon be facing important decisions about sex. To handle these well, they need to be able to recognize the difference between facts and value judgments. The best way we can help them is by making this difference clear in the things we say every day.

For practice, try deciding whether each of these statements is a value statement or a statement of fact. *(Hint: value statements often include one of these words — should, ought, good, bad, right, wrong.)*

"By the time they are 12, girls should get more interested in being pretty and ladylike." *(value judgment)*

"By the time they are 12, a lot of girls get more interested in being pretty and ladylike." *(fact)*

"A guy who has not started dating by the time he is 17 must be weird." *(value judgment)*

"Most people masturbate at some time during their lives." *(fact)*

"Nowadays, many people think it's okay to have intercourse before marriage." *(fact)*

"It's okay to have sex before marriage, if both people know what they are doing." *(value judgment)*

"When it comes to premature sex, it is worse for girls to do it than for guys." *(value judgment)*
(While it's a fact that only girls get pregnant, the word "worse" adds a judgment.)

"Many girls who have a baby while in high school never get a diploma." *(fact)*

QUESTIONS, QUESTIONS

Preteens probably will not ask direct questions about values. Still they may mention things that give you a chance to discuss your views. For instance, "Janie says when you're 13 you're old enough to go steady." Here is your opportunity to say what you believe about dating, and why you believe it. Your child may or may not agree with what you say right then. But if you can say it respectfully you will keep the door open for continued communication on this subject.

Preteens are very curious about their bodies and how they work. They do not always feel free to ask questions, however. Whether they ask or not, here are some of the things they often want to know:

When will I develop like my friends?
Why do kids say dirty words?
Why do babies look like their parents?
What causes twins? Siamese twins?
Why do some babies turn out to be boys and others, girls?
What happens to the sperm cells that don't fertilize the egg?
What about the eggs that don't get fertilized?
How does a baby stay alive inside the mother?
Why are some children adopted?
Why can't men have babies?
What's an abortion?
What does "making it," (or "getting down," etc.) mean?
What is oral sex? Is oral sex, sex?
What is a wet dream? Do girls have them?
What does "masturbation" mean?
What's a condom for?

What is a homosexual?
What are men's 'balls' for?
What are STDs (*sexually transmitted diseases*), AIDS, or herpes?
How do you catch it?
Does menstruation (or ejaculation, intercourse, or childbirth) hurt?
Do boys have periods?

It is perfectly normal for a preteen to be interested in these topics. Of course, some parents find that they do not know the answers to all of their child's questions. Many are answered in the front part of this book. For others you may wish to get more information in additional books or the Internet. We recommend having a good reference book on sexuality to keep at home. This gives the message that you want your child to get the right information, and that home is a place where questions can be answered. It should be a resource you are comfortable with and one you will be comfortable with your child having access to.

SEXUAL FEELINGS

Some parents worry that talking about sexuality – especially admitting that everyone has sexual feelings as they mature – will encourage children to experiment with sex too early. Quite the contrary! In fact, recognizing sexual feelings for what they are can help your soon-to-be-teenager resist being "swept away" in the heat of passion. Preteens need to be prepared in advance, so they can tell the difference between sexual feelings, peer pressure, and falling in love. It is much easier to start discussing these topics at this stage, before the moods and conflicts of adolescence begin.

In today's world young people already get plenty of messages telling them that sex feels good, or that it will make them feel grown-up. That is exactly why it is so important that they have parents who are willing to discuss the power of sexual feelings and the difference between feeling and doing.

Sexual orientation is another area of discussion that is appropriate with preteens. Statistics indicate that approximately 1 in 10 youths have a sexual preference for one of their own gender. Today most believe this is a predetermined part of a person's sexuality and that it does surface in preteen and teenage years. There seems to be a broad continuum between heterosexual and homosexual with many of us falling in various places along that line. Our society encourages us to be heterosexuals and that is certainly the orientation of most. You can still explain to your child that occasional feelings of attraction towards someone of their own gender does not mean they are gay or homosexual. Young teens need to understand what sexual orientation means, the appropriate terminology (including that which is disrespectful) and learn to be tolerant of individual differences among their peers.

HAZARDS AND RISKS

Sexuality education would not be complete without discussing risks, such as sexually transmitted diseases (including AIDS), unintended pregnancy, as well as the emotional upsets that can occur in relationships. This book begins the process by introducing the basic facts for pre-adolescents. It is intended to be a start for further learning.

Young people also need to know that sex raises the emotional risks of a relationship. While sex is often portrayed as "casual," few adolescents experience it this way. Adding sex to an immature relationship increases the risk of feeling hurt, jealous, smothered, or used. These painful feelings are often carried over into future relationships and affect those relationships negatively.

As you discuss these risks with your preteen or teenager, aim to keep a sense of balance. All too often, sexuality education has been a lesson in the "terrible things that can happen to you if you do it." Being able to talk about the positive as well as the negative aspects of sexuality will make you a more credible, "ask-able" parent. For pre-adolescents, a key message is that they can prevent serious problems by making sensible decisions, and eventually grow up to enjoy healthy, satisfying sexual lives.

The younger teens are when they first have sex, the more sexual partners they will have. Having multiple sexual partners without protection exposes an individual to more risk of STDs and unintended pregnancy and fatherhood.

COMMON SEXUALLY TRANSMITTED DISEASES (STDs)

Sexually transmitted diseases may be one of the most overlooked health problems in America. The cause of STDs may be a virus, a parasite or bacteria, depending on the individual infection. Most STDs occur during the age range of teens through 20s, mainly because this age group is more likely to have multiple sexual partners, have sex with someone who has had multiple sexual partners, or engaged in unprotected sex.

Adolescents need to know about the specific sexual activities that can transmit these infections (in addition to knowing these can be transmitted by sharing needles to shoot drugs). These include vaginal, oral and anal sex. These forms of sexual activity are fairly common among adolescents but often are ignored by well meaning parents who feel uncomfortable discussing them. Today, it is common among a large segment of teens to engage in oral sex and believe that it is perfectly safe because there is no risk of pregnancy. However, there IS a significant risk for sexually transmitted diseases during oral sex (for both partners) and ANY unprotected acts. Keep in mind that the ways STDs are transmitted differ somewhat from one disease to the next. For instance, genital warts and herpes can be transmitted by genital contact with an infected person, with or without intercourse. It is important for adolescents to know about STDs and how to protect themselves.

ANY person who engages in unprotected sex may contract a STD. Even though statistics may indicate that the rate of sexual activity among teens is declining, the rate of sexually transmitted diseases remains high. 1 in 4 teens will contract a STD. It is also important for kids to know that many individuals who have a STD may not show any symptoms and may not even be aware that they have contracted one. Going to a doctor or clinic is how you diagnose a STD.

It is critical for parents to educate themselves about sexually transmitted diseases. Some common STDs in the United States include:

- Genital HIV (Human papillomavirus)
- Trichomoniasis
- Chlamydia
- External Genital Warts
- Genital Herpes
- Gonorrhea
- HIV/AIDS
- Syphilis

Specific information about symptoms, what can happen if untreated (such as infertility) and how the diseases are transmitted can be obtained from your doctor, clinic, your local Planned Parenthood or on websites listed on page 88. It is important to know that all STDs have treatments. <u>It is important to diagnose and treat any infection EARLY so that further or more serious health problems that may affect an individual for life may be avoided.</u>

HOW STDS (AND PREGNANCY) ARE PREVENTED

The simple answer —"abstinence"— is a strong start. Young people certainly need adult support and sound reasons for abstaining from sexual activities. The front section of this book opens the door for talking about these matters.

Eventually, though, nearly everyone has a sexual relationship and must deal with these risks. For many, sexual experimentation begins in the early teen years. Although your pre-adolescent may seem young for a discussion of safer sex, the information is more easily and effectively conveyed ahead of time — before there is a specific partner in the picture. Statistics indicate that 1 out of 5 teens have had sex by the age of 15. Your discussion of prevention should include a description of how to obtain and use condoms, contraceptives, spermicides, or other forms of prevention or protection.

Studies show that condoms are 98% to 100% effective at preventing HIV/ AIDS and substantially decrease the risk of infection with other STDs.

Some parents worry that this information may encourage sexual activity. However, an early adolescent can easily understand a two-tiered message: "We've talked about some of the reasons why it's better to wait to have sex. But I want you to know how to protect yourself, even if you don't use the information for quite a while." Unfortunately, using abstinence as the only lesson has proven to be ineffective.

THE INTERNET

A whole new world — both helpful and dangerous — is now available to children online. Explore parental controls and filters that may be available to you and your computer. Let your children know that there are predators who like to take advantage of youth online. Preteens should not respond to people they don't know. Keeping computers that children access in a family room (versus their bedrooms) will help you manage how your child uses the computer. Sexual innuendo email names are to be avoided for kids. Just as you teach children how to safely respond to a phone call, let them know that personal information should not be shared with anyone they don't know by email or even at a website.

KEEPING THE DISCUSSION ONGOING

There are several reasons to continue your parent-child discussion of these issues into the teenage years. First, more detailed information will be appropriate for your maturing teenager, after he or she learns the basics. What they don't learn from trusted adults, they will learn from their peers and often what they learn from peers is wrong. Second, repeated information is more likely to be retained. And, finally, "current" information is continually changing, as new medical findings, tests, and treatments appear. Up-to-date pamphlets and videos, available from your county health department or local Planned Parenthood organization, can be especially valuable in covering these topics. (See the reading list and websites at the end of this section.) You need to be sure your young teens are familiar with the risks that can affect the rest of their lives.

One final note. Two groups of young people merit special attention: those who think they may be gay and those who have a family member infected by HIV. Both can benefit from additional support and information, beyond the scope of this book. To find out about counseling or support groups, check with your local AIDS service organization or mental health agency.

...AND IF THEY DON'T ASK

Because sex is so rarely discussed openly in families, many children learn not to bring up the subject with their own parents. What do you do if your child does not ask?

Here are some ideas that have worked for other parents:
• Show that it's okay to talk about sexual issues by talking with your spouse or other adults when the children are around. Include teens or pre-teens in the discussion when appropriate.
• Go to one of the movies your children go to, watch one of their TV shows, or listen to their music. This can open the door to discussions of sex and

values. If you disapprove of messages you see or hear, tell your children politely what it is about these messages that you don't like.

• Comment on sex-related events in everyday life. If your children notice a pregnant friend, or show curiosity about tampons or other personal products, that is a good starting point for talking about reproduction or menstruation.

A FEW THINGS NOT TO DO

• Don't tell them, "You're not old enough to know about that." This comment gives the message that you are not willing to discuss this, and perhaps other sensitive subjects. If they are already thinking about any topic, then they need correct information about it, in terms appropriate to their age.

• When talking about everyday things, don't make comments that are too harsh or too general. Too many statements like "Look at her — that's disgusting!" can turn off further discussion. It is better to be less negative and more specific: "She is a pretty woman, but I don't think the grocery store is the right place to wear a bikini." This type of statement tells your children more about your values.

• Don't tease them about their changing bodies and feelings, and don't allow other family members to tease them either. Such teasing only adds pain and alienation at a time when most youngsters are already very sensitive.

• Don't use too much humor when you talk about sex. Humor, at the right time, can help to relieve embarrassment. But if most of your talk is in the form of jokes, your children may get the message that sex is not a subject you are willing to talk about seriously.

WHEN NOT TO TALK ABOUT SEX

Yes, there are times to wait before having these discussions. It is better not to talk with your child about sex if such conversations seem too tense and unpleasant for your child.

Do not try to carry on a discussion:
   • When in a public place or their friends are there.
   • When you are in the middle of a family argument or crisis.
   • When you are extremely embarrassed, disgusted, or fearful about sex. You might need to talk first to a close friend or counselor about your feelings.
   • When you are experiencing sexual problems in your marriage and there is anger and conflict surfacing daily. Again, it may be better to wait until you have resolved your own problems before talking with your child.
   • When your child STRONGLY refuses to do so, or appears extremely nervous or feels sick. You can try again later.

Such an extreme reaction could possibly be a sign that your child has been sexually abused. If you suspect that abuse has actually occurred, the way you respond can make a big difference. You might gently assure your child that it is safe to tell you if anything happened, even if someone has warned, "don't tell your parents." *(Indicate that you believe what your child is saying or at least listen without commenting or negating what your child is telling you.)* Be as calm and matter-of-fact as possible. Reassure your child that you still love her or him as much as before. Finally, find a good counselor for your child to talk with. (Your local rape counseling center can suggest qualified professionals.)

WHEN YOU WANT TO THINK ABOUT YOUR ANSWER

Not every question has to be answered immediately. It is certainly okay to wait if, for instance, your child asks about tampons in the grocery checkout line. You might say, "Let's talk about that when we get home," or "I'd like to give that a little thought." Then be sure that you do follow up without waiting to be asked again.

WHAT DO YOU HOPE TO ACCOMPLISH?

By using this book you can give children basic facts about sex that will take away unnecessary fears and worries. By talking together, day-by-day, you can give them a clearer idea of what your family believes. You may enjoy a greater feeling of trust because your children will know that you are willing to talk about even difficult subjects.

Do you expect that your children will discuss all their sexual concerns with you? It probably will not happen. No matter how good your relationship is, your teenagers will probably choose to keep some things to themselves, or maybe share them only with their friends. That is a normal part of growing up. But if you have shown that you are willing to talk, and to listen, they are more likely to make responsible decisions, and to ask for your advice when they really need it.

In sexual matters, as in everything else, your children will ultimately have to make their own decisions. Naturally you want to help them avoid unwise choices. You also want to help them understand that sex can be a very important and satisfying part of their lives. By making sure that they have correct information, a clear idea of your beliefs, and plenty of chances to communicate with you are giving them the best possible start in this direction.

WEBSITES FOR PARENTS

Planned Parenthood/ Mar Monte
www.ppmarmonte.org

Planned Parenthood Federation of America
www.plannedparenthood.org
American Social Health Association
www.ashastd.org

SIECUS/Sexuality Information & Educational Council
www.siecus.org (go to: parent information)

PFLAG/Parents, Families & Friends of Lesbians and Gays
www.pflag.org

Advocates for Youth
www.advocatesforyouth.org

National Campaign to Prevent Teen Pregnancy
http://www.thenationalcampaign.org

Center for Disease Control
www.cdc.gov

Coalition for Positive Sexuality
www.positive.org

ADDITIONAL BOOKS FOR PARENTS

EVERYTHING YOU NEVER WANTED YOUR KIDS TO KNOW ABOUT SEX BUT WERE AFRAID THEY'D ASK: THE SECRETS TO SURVIVING YOUR CHILD'S DEVELOPMENT FROM BIRTH TO TEENS
by Dr. J. Richardson and Dr. M. Schuster (Crown, 2003)

HOW TO TALK TO YOUR CHILD ABOUT SEX: IT'S BEST TO START EARLY BUT IT'S NEVER TOO LATE
by Linda and Richard Eyre (St. Martins, 1999)

FROM DIAPERS TO DATING: A PARENT'S GUIDE TO RAISING SEXUALLY HEALTHY CHILDREN
by Debra Hoffner (Newmarket, 2004)

KEYS TO YOUR CHILD'S HEALTHY SEXUALITY
by Chrystal De Freitas (Barrons, 1998)

HOW TO TALK SO KIDS WILL LISTEN AND LISTEN SO KIDS WILL TALK
by Adele Faber Elaine Mazlish (Avon, 1999)

TEN TALKS PARENTS MUST HAVE WITH THEIR CHILDREN ABOUT SEX AND CHARACTER
by Pepper Schwartz (Hperion, 2000)

STRAIGHT PARENTS, GAY CHILDREN
by Robert Bernstein (Thunder's Mouth Press, 2003)

Published by Book Peddlers

PERIOD.
A Girl's Guide
with a Parent's Guide

by Joanne Loulan and Bonnie Worthen
illustrated by Marcia Quackenbush and Chris Dyrud
100 pages • 7" x 7" • 75 line drawings • $9.99

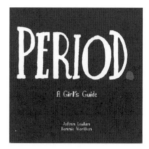

This bestselling, illustrated book about menstruation has been revised and updated for this new generation of young women. It will be passed on by the previous 200,000 women who came through puberty thanks to this groundbreaking book first published in 1979.

Written with the younger girl in mind, this book contains no sex education.

Here is everything a young girl needs to know to prepare for her own body's changes.

"PERIOD. is THE rite-of-passage guide that all parents should give to their daughters. The Parent's Guide is its indispensable companion for family communication." — Vicki Lansky,
parenting author

" Reassuring, cleverly illustrated book about menstruation explaining why all girls are normal and at the same time everyone is special." — Siecus Report

"A fine, friendly, supportive, right-on book...I love your voice, your clarity, your wholistic approach." — Wendy Sanford, co-author, OUR BODIES, OURSELVES

Also available in Spanish:
PERIODO. Lo que su hija debe saber $9.99

— ORDER FORM —

FOR ADDITIONAL COPIES

contact your local bookstore or :

Book Peddlers, 18925 Lake Ave, Deephaven, MN 55391
952-544-1154
www.bookpeddlers.com

Please send:

_____ copies of **LET'S TALK ABOUT S-E-X** at $9.99 each = _____

_____ copies of *HABLEMOS ACERCA DEL S-E-X-O* at $9.99 each = _____

_____ copies of **PERIOD. A Girl's Guide** at $9.99 each = _____

_____ copies of *PERIODO. Lo que su hija debe saber* at $9.99 each = _____

Shipping: Add $4.00 for first book and 50 cents for each additional book.
All orders must be prepaid. Make checks or money orders
payable to *Book Peddlers* or pay by *VISA or Master Card.*

TOTAL _____

credit card #: _____ expiration date: _____

Name *(as it appears on the card):* _____

Signature for credit card: _____

Ship To:
Name/Organization_____

Address_____

City _____ State _____ Zip_____

Telephone ( ) _____ Fax ( ) _____

Email _____

Agencies, schools, medical professionals and organizations may qualify
for discounts on purchases of these titles.
For further information, please contact Book Peddlers at the address above.